IN THE DARK

RUTH STONE

In the Dark

 COPPER CANYON PRESS

Cover art: *CHI* by Carolyn Heryford Watts, oil on canvas, courtesy of the artist.

Copper Canyon Press is in residence at Fort Worden State Park in Port Townsend, Washington under the auspices of Centrum Foundation. Centrum is a gathering place for artists and creative thinkers from around the world, students of all ages and backgrounds, and audiences seeking extraordinary cultural enrichment.

LIBRARY OF CONGRESS CATALOGING-IN-PUBLICATION DATA

Stone, Ruth.
In the dark / Ruth Stone.
    p. cm.
ISBN 1-55659-210-8 (alk. paper)
1. People with visual disabilities – Poetry.   2. Loss (Psychology) –
Poetry.   3. Aging – Poetry.   I. Title.
PS3537.T6817I53 2004
811'.54 – DC22

                                                    2004006039

9 8 7 6 5 4 3 2
FIRST PRINTING

COPPER CANYON PRESS
Post Office Box 271
Port Townsend, Washington 98368
www.coppercanyonpress.org

Lovingly dedicated to my daughter, Marcia Stone Croll,
and my granddaughter, poet Nora Swan Croll,
who were my eyes for many months, reading aloud,
transcribing from my notebooks, discussing,
organizing, typing and proofreading *In the Dark*.

Contents

IN THE DARK

Accepting

Half-blind, it is always twilight.
The dusk of my time and the nights
are so long, and the days of my tribe
flash by, their many-colored cars
choking the air, and I lie like a shah
on my divan in this 21st century
mosque, indifferent to my folded
flesh that falls in on itself,
almost inert, remembering crossing
the fields, turning corners, coming
home to the lighted windows,
the pedestrian years of it, accepting
from each hand the gifts,
without knowing why they were
given or what to make of them.

Another Day

The fleeting high that lifts you
at six AM after a cup of coffee;
or is it that you've lived into another day?
After the sun sets and you look out there
on the dark that is neither down nor up,
not even the patterns of stars can tell you where.

Still, light comes and lies on your skin
like the membrane of a delicate egg.
You do not need to feel anything,
enclosed in this sac: etched lineage,
ball of twine, fractal of lost feathers.

Another Feeling

Once you saw a drove of young pigs
crossing the highway. One of them
pulling his body by the front feet,
the hind legs dragging flat.
Without thinking,
you called the Humane Society.
They came with a net and went for him.
They were matter of fact, uniformed;
there were two of them,
their truck ominous, with a cage.
He was hiding in the weeds. It was then
you saw his eyes. He understood.
He was trembling.
After they took him, you began to suffer regret.
Years later, you remember his misfit body
scrambling to reach the others.
Even at this moment, your heart
is going too fast; your hands sweat.

Full Moon

My problem is not enough
or too much sleep;
uneasy sleep, apnea sleep.
Is it the hole in the ozone?
That snooze effect?
Another full moon,
our divided self,
out there baring
its hard flesh.
The spotlight
on the world's goiter;
the gland that affects
our tidal blood.
Every river vein
lifts like an eyebrow
with the pull.
A globe fish
pronged in weeds;
black stiff hairs
against the blind sky.
The hemlocks, the woods,
a rising slope;
matte wig of the mountain.
The evening birds
diving from branch to branch;
or full spread, a nightjar,
ready to throttle
to another nightjar.

An Imprint of the Roaring Twenties

I have a weakness for grubbing at the Salvation Army's discard tables:
old sheets, halves of curtains, soiled pillows,
sometimes a quaint hand-embroidered cardtable cloth
like the ones my cousin Frances used
when her three young, married, and in-trouble friends
gathered in her bungalow living room
trading their sorrows, their silver liquor flasks,
the stories of their dismal bedroom suites.

Frances served desserts with whipped cream.
Her women friends spent almost every morning in her bungalow,
playing cards and comparing their men.
The ashtrays were emptied and filled again and again.
Two of the women had not yet bobbed their hair.
Just before noon they would gather up the cards
(they gambled for cash)
and spread the starched ironed tablecloth,
like a dead body for viewing. They all helped.
They knew the routine. Frances's tea towels,
exquisite crossed-stitched hand-hemmed linen,
hung in her kitchen only for display.
The dingy rags she really wiped her dishes with
were hidden under the sink.

When I was fourteen, and still imprinting like a baby duck,
I went with Frances to visit one of these friends.
She banged the knocker.
We waited a considerable time for an answer.

Finally the friend barely cracked open the door.
She was wiping her face with her apron.
Her eyes were swollen almost shut,
she was incoherent, her manner distraught.
She didn't invite us in.
We went away, Frances saying, "It's Jim.
He's left her for that slut. She thought
they were just trading partners again."

Like the others, Frances got divorced.
Her husband, Joe, was an alcoholic bookkeeper
in the office of the Norfolk and Western.
So she married a richer, older railroad man,
but he died a few years after
(mean-mouthed relatives said she drove him to it)
and Frances drank herself into senility.

She fell into bouts of paranoia. The family
refused to answer when she knocked.
The nursing home where she was sent
gradually acquired her bungalow and other assets.
I suppose someone got the wicker furniture, the tea towels,
and the cardtable-size embroidered tablecloths.

Becoming Vegetarian

Slowly I am pulling my teeth.
Now I am only drinking water.
You grass eaters with two stomachs,
let me be a stippled shadow
where you lie down, your sweet breath
unlike the sulfur of volcanoes.

I came devouring my mother.
Now I drip tears like icicles in March.
I push my cart of rags crying, "No carrion."

Bennington Bus Stop

She gets off the bus and they kiss.
It's a hard embrace.
Then he walks on the balls of his feet
like a basketball star,
and contorts himself into the driver's
seat of a compact car.
She stands outside,
averts her face,
wipes her lips with the back of her hand
as if to erase a smear,
or a breath of dust on a photograph
album stacked in the future.
Then she slips into her place
beside him and everything is sure
as the weekend, as sure
as their nineteen-year-old bodies,
as sure as death
that sweetens their given grace.

Body Language

Across from the hospital,
interns and student nurses order fish sandwiches.
A pyramid of vitamins, endorsed by Olympic teams,
in the flyspecked window. Surgically impersonal,
the manager removes his jacket and sits, watching
from an elevated position in the plywood office.
The newly discharged patient reaches down
to bring an overnight valise under her feet.
In the mirror, she sees herself at the counter.
Flaking gray letters on the glass intrude across her shocked face.
She pushes a paper cup of water like a quoit, or the end of a thought.
Two doctors, identical mustaches
on their upper lips, order black coffee.
They assume an exaggerated medical *par nobile fratrum*
for the benefit of the interns.
The patient holds her pocketbook stuffed with toiletries
from the hospital bed stand. She stares
for a long hypnotic moment at the enamel nose of a male urinal.

Bianca

On the cement belt over the cement playground,
buses, cars, trucks, move from one side
to the other. Hyphens of traffic;
dashes from nowhere to nowhere.
We sit on the benches under the sycamore.

And in the almost indestructible play-yard,
Bianca finds a throng of dandelions.
Her tenderness gathers them up.
Her yellow hair hanging over them,
her astringent herbal essence.
Her small hands filling passion's bitter cup.

Walter, Upon Looking Around

"Men are getting extinct,"
says my grandson, Walter.
"Look how little I am;
and I'm the only boy in the family.
I hardly ever see a boy,"
he says, warming to his subject.

Between Men

My memories of the Johnstown flood
are not as clear as my received
impressions of the Holocaust.
My mother was in utero.

The dam broke, the water rushed
in minutes into Williamsport;
grandmother tying a rope
around grandfather's waist,
grandfather swimming to the barn
to turn the horses out.
The flood rose to their second floor.

When they were putting in the Erie Canal
my grandparents met.
My great-grandfather was the overseer.
His daughter, my grandmother, was cooking for the crew.
One day my grandfather came along looking for a job.
Perhaps he hung around because of her.
He was an elegant man and a connoisseur
of women, lots of women.
And quick and skillful with his wits and hands.
My great-grandfather looked the other way.
She was not a virgin, but a widow.
So without consulting his daughter,
he let him know he could have her.
It was a small matter. It was just between men.

A Male Tale

Once a cat named Cripes left home to do something good for the world. He had an idea. "Things would be better," he said, "if there were more cats like me." He was shiny and young and had brand-new gonads. "Whoa out there," he said under his breath. He had a real for-sure swagger. "No more chasing plastic balls down halls for me," he said to himself.

Winter lay fresh all over the houses and lawns, white and crystal. The stale odor of another Christmas hung in the air like soot. The mailperson was weighted down with flyers from Wal-Mart. All of the known colors were printed on slick paper. The forests nearby smelled their dead relatives and stood at attention.

Cripes was looking for a convert. Someone to pass on the word. He had been born in a barn. A significant event. But that had fallen down. "Where are the outcasts now?" he said. "Where are my brothers and sisters? Momma mia, where is my mother? I must spread the word!" cried Cripes.

How far the twinkle of streetlights and the Doppler shift of red taillights. The shadows of old beaten horses stood about him. "My father is the great mysterious All, and I am his son." And he rushed into the dark, freighted with seeds of wisdom and love. And the trees wept, for none of them wanted to be the cross.

Calibrate

How happy am I
to apply
this brief kiss,
or can I say,
today I am a woman,
perhaps clay,
perhaps human.

Rushing along the galaxy,
this string bag of easy puzzles.

To make matters worse,
I'm happy.
Calibrate:
A veil of wet snow,
a diffuse sun,
there are the planks of the porch,
there is the wooden rail,
there are the willow whips
like Desdemona's hair,
or Lear's blind tears
beyond recall.

Clay

Tuesday and I am still in the coils
of this serpent masking as a vein.
It has swallowed so much. I am the half-
swallowed toad still kicking in the throat.

It's like I walk to the end of the world
and come to a wall. There is no top to the wall.
It goes up forever. My body adds itself to the bricks.

Cause and Effect

Once a stick who was tired
of being beaten against everything
lay down on the fagot pile.
"Let me ascend to heaven," it snarled.
Presently wood smoke rose
from the poet's chimney.

Chausible Plausible

The souls of your feet are saints
of coarse calloused rough weave,
the mock piety of the absurd.
"Here," you shout down to them.
"Pray get on with it."
They move, after a pause.
The electric message relayed
from the altar, as it were;
where your voice echoes
in the chambers and vaults
under the Art Nouveau stained glass
windows of your vested self.

Border

Driving through Indiana,
creeks wriggle alongside the highway,
incidental,
like, "Oh yes,
someone used to wade there."
A knot of deformed trees,
almost too old-fashioned,
remnants of a farm, discontinued merchandise.
But it's mostly lost streams,
weed-trees, and a loneliness that hints
of automatic two-car-garage doors and zoysia grass;
small, well kept lawns and sudden streets,
and identical houses around a factory
that sprawls the way small colleges used to spread themselves out:
lawns, flower beds, groundsmen with mowing machines.
The quiet authority of culture.

Am I

I am outside the Boston Psychopathic.
I ascend to the third floor and look in a window.
Dennis Leigh, neurosurgeon and Freudian analyst,
is sitting at his desk. He has my case.
Later in a suburb of London he will say over the phone,
when I tell him my husband has hung himself,
"Well, what do you want me to do about that?"
His wife explains that it is his arthritis
that makes him so irritable.
The suicide had nothing to do with international crisis.
His death came between wars.
He may have identified with Keats (owls, nightingales,
Hampstead Heath), but it was only a rooming house.
The problem with all this is, first I saw the psychiatrist,
then the events. Did he die before or afterward?
However, the doctor played tennis.
The window overlooks the Atlantic. The porthole
is open. The mineral air, so good for you.
Or in the ship's bar, queezy, listening, with the swell,
you smell the spar varnish.
How inadequate; right out of the avenues
of Indianapolis, running in from the outskirts,
you seem to have brought Mr Vogule along with you.
He was the grade-school janitor from Switzerland
who had a tobacco-yellowed mustache
and danced and sang and slept by the furnace
and shoveled the path through the snow
to the girls' outdoor toilet. See, you say,

that was easy. The doctor knows you are there.
He is making his English effort to be severe with
your attractive body. You are sitting across from him
in the patient's chair. By now he will be seventy or dead.
He gave you bad advice. The usual educated, ignorant,
British male practice. If you looked quickly, you could
see his slight smile go slack. All the time his wife
was secretly calling him from overseas. Someone
wanted him for handball. "Am I crazy?" you asked an intern
late the first night in the sterilized room;
your personality like moth wings, shredding itself
on the hospital furniture. "I don't know," he said.
It was a hard fact.

Consider This

It means you have to breathe it in, inhale;
become cell by cell a polymer;
transfer your basic and parasitical formula
(at one time a worm which grew from crystals;
in fact, probably from clay… sound familiar?)
chemical by chemical.
And here's the difference:
Plastic is firm, practical.
Flesh was subject to decay.
Plastic can be manufactured and parts replaced.
This is the solution for us. No waste!
Gross national products guarantee eternity.
From the first plastic heart to the olyester
blood bank and viral-resistant peel-proof skin.
Ovaries ready to ovulate! Up-front sperm!

Almost the Same

When it's all over,
the ravishing lines,
the simple innuendos,
something implied beyond the self.
As if like the jewelweed
you have scattered yourself
God knows where,
and you are positioned to be a silhouette
against the snow.
And where is this poem going,
if not into stasis?
All words on stone or papyrus,
linen or pulp,
written in some loved alphabet,
thousands of years old.
Scribes, and the counting for taxes,
or the river's seasonal flooding.
Ships drifting,
and the same, or
almost the same
sun.

Currents

Something about a flock of birds toward evening.
The weather report sleet, snow.
The hot males riding ahead,
the swamp ridged in last year's cattails.
Ego, vanity, the male strut.
Oh, that burr and sweetest whistle,
their hearts pumped with thrush steroids.
In another week, perhaps a quick melt
and we'll hear them clinging to the old stalks,
staking out their claims
while from the south
the slow shadow of the migrating females
like Cleopatra's barge,
the oars dipping,
the fringed canopy
like clouds of sweet rain
rippling behind.
The eternal tribal ritual,
the dense flock, undulating
packet of the future –
great sperm bank of the galaxy,
the billions of the separate
that gathers itself into the one,
summer after summer.

Fragrance

Love, linked to procreation, to survival;
Self, that in old age desires to bloom
like the century plant, the cactus;
nevertheless, when the floods of sorrow come,
mouth open, hands wax, and the half-shut eyes,
belonging to that hammock in which we nest,
hole in the ground all fractured and rearranged
as even continents and oceans. Not a room,
not a corridor; each cell breaks into another
as a violated ship of the night, the lungs of the invader
sucking in the elusive esters, the fragrance
that waited for resurrection evaporating;
the fragile, elusive fragrance of longing.

Always Icarus

What can we know?
These enormous simplicities
we ask ourselves.
From a great distance
we wait for the glue to stick.
Stopped in flight, the navigator
of the plane, whose designs
overrode the myth of angels,
his voice on the black box
saying, "Oh, shit,"
when the wing dropped off.

Elsie's Brooks

It's hard to carry you around inside me
without the real sound of your voice
that was not always praising me,
and did I say enough to you
concerning those peripheral things
I knew you cared about?
The lazy time was lazy in my voice.
There were so many silences.
I think, do you hear me now
speaking for both of us?
Thinking along those paths
you walked more often alone,
going up in the woods behind your house
and farther up, where you found
blue hepatica, bone white trillium,
and the source of the springs
that had spread out down the slope
in a broad swamp. You worked the water free
of years of rot and silt and dug those brooks
back to their rock beds where now the clear
water runs down hill. Your muddy wet
tennis shoes were always lined up
on the porch where you would come
down to change out of one soaked
and mud-filled pair into a dry mud-caked
replica, and after a cup of tea, you'd go
back up there to drain the mountain.

Eta Carinae

Am I the ears, the nose, the lobes,
the mouth, the eyes,
or just the teeth and touch?
It isn't much. Worms,
the nematodes and such
are just as well equipped.
And where are we now, old darkness?
We've slipped across the last galactic heaven.
Rough gas, dust, Rigel,
Betelgeuse and the Dog Star.
What use are they to me? I am no sailor.
Yet the round worm, the flat worm,
and the nematode persist.
And who knows,
another crossing the lanes of dust,
and the center of the flower
against the walls of fire,
the jewel box.

So

Today, which could be tomorrow
or next week,
we passed through the unified
feel theory.
"Feel me," was what it said.
And it meant it like rose, lilac,
lily, and mint.
"Not I," says me, considering
the size of the knotgrass
pretending to be grass.
"I'll feel none of you."
However, I took a deep breath.
Since the hoe was in my hands,
I dug. And forth came worms,
halved and quartered.
I said, "Death, you breed
in every clod, and you
ask us to do your dirty work."

And So Forth

Someone, or a group of someones,
has gone to consider the strange altered behavior
of penguins along the tip of South America.
It's a film and reporting thing to do.
And someone like me thinks upon it.
Here in darkest Binghamton, I think of the plight of penguins
in the rapidly changing climate
of the oceans and polar regions.
As even now, lightning flashes in mid-December,
and rain and ice coat the glistening asphalt.
This small polluted cluster of towns,
spawned by the shoemaking industry.
Many fat people,
their genes programmed to make fat,
waddle about the streets of these now
mall-dominated towns.
And shoes are made overseas.
The World Wide Web is absolutely nothing,
multiplied by what seems to be an infinite number.
As we swing upon it, filling its no-space
with our so-called communications,
we are filled with the almost perfect vacuum
of nothing at all.
But as an Adélie penguin becomes my own penguin,
inside my skull, even its oil-coated sleek body
that stands and waddles toward its own nest,
somewhere among the million other nests,
and its own chick crying out

among the million others, is distinctive.
Can I hope the great ear of the universe
is pressed to the wall of space and hears me,
its own chick, peeping? Over here in this galaxy,
this welter of debris and gases,
rushing along this arm of rock and stars,
this little freight of penguins
and so forth?

Cosmos

Let me speak as a grasshopper to the universe,
rebounding, always rebounding.
Where do we leap,
old mother?
The air is filled with your progeny.
The dissolving suns
what scars they cut,
and yet, the ones that blew apart were gathered in
like spider's silk.
What is this speech, this blind fingering of the dark?
Nothing, old mother,
but your wasted breath.

Exotic Extras for Reading at City College

After the carnival bump-the-bumps,
I mean the Mack Sennett chase
in the New York cab;
the dive into suddenly
separating cross-country trucks,
just missing the sides of buildings, dogs,
off the curb, and the Brooklyn Bridge,
at dissolving speeds;
after a night of chill, since you
couldn't figure the heating system buttons,
suspecting they were decoys;
you are being obsequiously served
the continental breakfast
in the dining area of the downtown
Holiday Inn, by the suavest of the suave,
those melting, boneless, exquisite, yet
fleshy, Chinese men at their most
charming when you feel like the Empress
Dowager in her mad later years,
all you can eat with rice for six-ninety-five,
and their tonal language – everything
is suddenly Chinese, the decor, the
mandarin robe altered to black suit
and tie, the formal funereal disquieting
preparation for your ludicrous bier upstairs
in the familiar blare and garish flicker
of your American TV stations but
not of course the actual TV

which, as we all know, in our greed
and sloth, was put together by women
and children in Taiwan. After all this,
which tomorrow will balloon into
the hyperspace of language, what is
ordinary, daily, expected, not even
expensive for those who live here,
you will shrink back into the Burger King
population of Binghamton, shoe city
of musical streets and boar-bristle mountains,
where also you will gratefully go
after a stressful day on the most laid-out
casual of campuses, to order from Wung Foo
a takeout of broccoli with garlic sauce,
all you can eat with rice for six-ninety-five.

Riding the Bubble

Poetry that uses non sequiturs
which are transformations
in the direction of Zen,
as the hyper-angle in Vasco
Popa's "Prudent Triangle" –
a linguistic arrangement
of infinity –
is intriguing to us

with our nearsighted vision
frozen along the contiguous;
our popular choice,
a self-inflating universe.

And so far, at the farthest
visible edge, the bubble appears
to bend; light appears to speed up
because it curves away from
where it was.

The still somewhat
unexplained weak force
possibly becoming aggregate;
separating masses,
galaxies slipping
out of sight in opposite directions.

Floaters

Today, through black floaters,
because my right eye is under siege
by that best-intentioned surgeon with laser,
today is thinly veiled.
And the sky with its black floaters
seems half-blind, too;
the crows dipping over the town.

October's brilliance is half gone from the avenues,
or lies on lawns and gutters;
and rain, the blessed curse
in dissolved frost, yields ropes of mirrors.
The cheap, chiming clock says almost ten.

Then why this happiness in muted things?
Some equation of time and space,
a slowed perception of the battered brain
strips back like leaves to unexpected glittering.

From Outer Space

Your gray glasses are for playing the piano.
Your brown glasses, for strong reading.
Birds scratch in the snow for seeds.
Your oldest cat sleeps on your best papers.
It is overcast, Tuesday, and the coffee
too dark. Nothing but sugar in the cupboard.
That's when the voice from the galaxy
comes back saying, praise be, it had a good
sleep; it is ready to translate. And the disc
that someone planted in your skull picks
up a little static and you hear, "...come in Minus
103. The Japanese report remnants, debris,
gas, large chunks of matter. Listen, listen,
I kid you not. This is real. Now get this down.
This morning, snow fell. Thirty-six blue jays,
fifteen assorted sparrows, and five surviving
chickadees fought through the weather.
Get this. A poem about a new subject, a fresh
approach. Now listen, write this down, we..."

The Self and the Universe

This is not poetic language,
but it is the language of poetry.
At night, on the page,
the lines change
like the chaotic patterns of your eyes,
these holes into space.
You lie on your bed,
the snowball earth,
a frozen chance;
the little knowledge of dust lanes,
the ghastly voter frauds of the last election,
and the late spring snows,
pots of forced purple crocuses.
How fragile and enduring the words.
This is the self and the universe.
This is the wild sweep of the sun,
that mysterious molecule;
this clutter of rocks, dust,
and lighter elements, like your fingernails;
like the configurations of the spiral lines
on the soles of your feet,
undeciphered.

Heaven

Before we knew the true
polyhedral vision
and reduced all possibility
to a perfectly fulfillable eternity;
ignorance hung
like a bat of viscous glue;
upside down –
beautiful blind insectivore.

Fear of the Doppelgänger

You are sure that the man
who so earnestly pursues you
with questions comes here because
after the reading there is food.
He eases along the table of cookies
and foam cups. If you listen he will
tell you that he also printed books
but in another country. Now he
writes in English. He asks for exact
information. How to apply for grants.
How to publish. How to pay for such
texts. And he eats.
You can't prove he has devised
this strategy to survive but you suspect.
He makes a joke about coming
from a one-donkey family.
On the bus going home, counting
your change, you remember his
large plastic teeth, a subliminal smell
of mold in his continental suit.
His gesture, draping a string scarf
across his throat, continues to give
you pain. And that sinking feeling returns.

Ice

Are you persuaded that dormant flies, moles,
bears, and all the rest, as the wheel slows down,
are as we, in the interstices of love? There toll
the small bells of their sleeping souls. We
do not sleep. We die and are reborn and die again,
as the annual flowers, in the pulse of pain.

Love, for a bridge of sighs, from my winter to yours,
to hang with icicle garlands that the wind may crash
and clang among. Then in our death's time, showers
of cold roses and snow poppies and the tracery of blue-white
forget-me-nots carved of the purest ice may lash
us with the sting of memory.

How Can I?

Saying it over and over,
the eyes forget
the subtle alphabet,
or calligraphy,
the sweet nuances of style,
and fall to hieroglyphics.
And the body, asleep,
walks along the Nile
planting papyrus,
a basket to catch words;
the feet caked with dust,
the poor thighs heavy,
and the entire torso squat,
not anyone you would remember.
And yet,
far away, lying on a foam mat,
the blind self thinks
how can I live like this?

I Walk Alone

Along the street at night,
sometimes the rain;
its bodiless déjà vu,
random street,
the rain's velvet scrim.
Almost the whisper of your voice,
as I remember
your elegant fingers
in the flare of a match
as we paused on the edge
of that illusion
that now rises from the dead,
that returns years from then
without warning,
on this dark street
where I stand transfixed,
embraced, but only by the wind.

In the Arts

In the Villa Montalvo gardens,
a bride under a white cowl, stiff as plaster,
stands for her wedding portrait.
Acacia, I say to myself, acacia, acacia.
I am in my two rooms on the second floor,
minding my own business: poet in residence.
Photographer's models, thinner than nubile
centerfolds, pose on the Villa steps,
on marble benches with lion's paws,
by Adam and Eve whose primo sexual organs
are discreetly lost in marble embrace.
I watch an older man in boxing shorts,
his trainer timing his pace, going uphill
toward heart attack. Likewise, two fat men climb
fifty vertical steps. The gates are open
from eight to five. The parking lots are full.
Dormant ropes of wisteria snake over the colonnade.
The vulgarity of all this commerce cannot be missed.
But happily, I note another prospect.
In plain view of the gallery and well-dressed
lady volunteers, an almost naked couple
are getting it on in the center of the vista.

In the Free World

The teenager in for involvement
in murder and dismemberment
feels unjustly treated. He says,
"Why I never even got my driver's
license." He refers to his offense
as "catching his case." He feels
no remorse for burying the skinned
and beheaded female victim.

A short time ago it was only thirty,
but now for under a hundred dollars,
you can get a license enabling you
to legally sell weapons; handguns,
machine guns, you are an automatic
licensed dealer in automatics.

And the Mexican government,
after betraying the native Mexican
farmers, sends helicopters in
to bomb them and quell dissatisfaction.
It's quicker and maybe more humane
than just starving them. After
the insurrection, the dead Indians
lying in their own blood were found
to be carrying carved wooden guns,
just pieces of carved wood.

Infrared

I suppose we are like glowworms to the snowman.
Or without reason, we compare the temporary icicle
hanging from the eaves,
to the innocents hanging when the KKK swept through the South.
Images arrive and pass like our own rush along the gaseous arm.
The fat cells of our bodies, steaming puffs of noxious elements
extracted from our waste, and when your aura merges with mine,
a subliminal electrical storm like approaching galaxies,
and suns thrown out of orbit, and creatures, the father of genetics
would not have dreamed of, stream across the radius
of other dimensions, in the curled-up mystery of what might have been.

Inner Truth

At night, I, the gut, am at work.
While you flicker in your muscles,
I am making fat out of the earliest mud.
I have lived so long in the dark.

My kind will take me into themselves
where you have fallen in the slough of it,
into their mouths,
then shit me back to begin the circle again.

I sing this song; force of light
that blows apart the mightiest of stars,
think now on me,
the godhead of this earth.

Leap from a Footnote

Miss Rae Huffman of the American Mission
is mentioned in a footnote (some years after the fact)
as having "a more detailed vocabulary of the Nuer."
I imagine Miss Huffman, briefly noted,
in swamps and open savannas below the juncture of the Sobat,
the Bahr el Gazal, and the Nile, with perhaps only a guide
and two carriers from the settlement, wading and cutting
her way through tough fibrous growths, her head
tied up with netting: insects, venomous snakes, crocodiles.
She is taking extensive notes on the cattle-acquisitive Nilotic
herdsmen, those long-bodied, narrow-headed, dour cousins
of the more peaceful Dinka, against whom they wage
continous war and cattle-stealing.
In Miss Huffman's time, bargaining in bride-wealth
among those marginal subsisters often reached sixty head.
Consider her conversations in Nuer sounds,
concerning cows and oxen, he-goats and she-goats;
her exchanges with the Wut Ghok, man of cattle;
her judicious offering, in bags of tobacco, drawing forth stories, gossip,
herself without benefit of pharmaceuticals beyond quinine.
It was the elixir of scholarship tricked out in religious garments,
wherein a woman might work and reside: that small, precarious
African tribe and Miss Rae Huffman.
Does the footnote imply that she was there observing the women,
who squatted by cows stroking the undernourished udders,
milking single teats into narrow-mouthed gourds
balanced on their hips; that she went among
the leopard men in cattle camps, accepting their dung-coated cheese,

processed in ox urine; that she waded the tussets of millet
in the wet season; that she talked with the young boys tending stock
in the dry season; that she gathered language and myth
from the illusive Nuer, patient as their own millet reapers?
I can only guess. Her work has been digested and used to advantage.
She herself remains obscure.

Interim

Like the radiator that sits
in the kitchen passing gas;
like the mop with its head
on the floor, weeping;
or the poinsettia that pretends
its leaves are flowers;
the cheap paint peels
off the steamed walls.
When you have nothing to say,
the sadness of things
speaks for you.

Blizzard

Birds hunting food,
flocks in the air, wheel
above the metal Dumpster.
Nothing there. Pigeons
plump in drifts. The woman
who stirs the Dumpster
abandons her bent cart.
A white veil ripples
across the buildings.
A snow plow, scrawny
as an old man's neck,
like a squawking chicken,
jerks its yellow eye
in the shrouded parking lot.
Main Street traffic stops.
Power lines sag.
Power goes out.
From the dark window,
flashing red lights,
sirens passing slow
through the diaphanous
scarves of blowing crystals.
The shudder of spumes,
sprays of fine ice
against the building.
It blows under the main door,
fills up the entrance
to the first step

to the first floor.
A long arm of snow stretches
along the basement hall,
along the basement apartments
where the retired women
living on Social Security
are sitting smoking
in front of their dark TVs.
Holding your breath,
you stand at the window.
The phone is dead.
Snow hisses against the glass.
You shiver and feel your way
in the dark. At last the matches.
You waver with lit candle
to the pit of your bed and
like a hibernating animal,
unconscious, crawl in to safety.
Mindless, you sleep as you
did on your mother's breast.
Until the sun streams in
as through a cathedral window,
as if you are blessed after a flogging.
Not a bird in sight, not a sound.
Not a Thai has come out.
Their blinds pulled down,
thick snow on their metal steps,
mounded without tracks.

Their timed lives,
day shift and night shift,
their exchange of beds,
some leaving, some entering,
interrupted.
Only imagined sacks of rice
behind the now darkened window,
the window around the corner
in the Thai Recreation Restaurant
and Pool Hall. Only silence
like a glitch, like a pause
in abnormal breathing;
and the large, comfortable
casket of the snow.

Drought Again

Here is the grass, an army.
It thinks it is invincible
with its weapons underground;
blind roots tapping down,
shoving the squat rocks.
The rocks are secret as potatoes.
They squint in their gum-dirt sockets
and Geiger-count a tremble coming
inch by inch. They wait
to be pulverized.
What do they care
if it has not rained for thirty-nine days?

Euphoria

This euphoria,
this sunlight in February,
these lines to myself.
Not even the ivy that looped
across my bedroom window;
and what were those summer mornings?
One grows up in a brick house
on a winding street
in Indianapolis.
Wildflowers on the slope
behind the house, the elms,
and beyond that, the railroad
with its blinking lights
and long Doppler whistle
of the evening train.
Hepatica, dog-toothed violet,
spring beauties.
And the elms, that formed green arches
over the street all the way
to the Baptist Church,
and three long blocks
from my grandmother's.
That blue sky, that delicate wind.

Writer's Block

As the heart changes,
the blood in its ragged sleeves
accommodates. And the poem-
to-paper throbs less,
more erratically;
moves to shade of rocks.
A stern rapture.

What was unfolding vision
that swept to the edge,
that turned in space,
so that morning split
open the dark
(and the body, blessed
in its sweat, lay motionless),
now takes every thing in place
though altered.

This other beat occurs
and the ear hears it,
deep inside its almost
insect structure,
and the hand trembles,
and the three-dimensional
words in their electrical
circuits come to the gates
and find them locked.

Clotheslines

Lines yes, clotheslines,
where the laundry lashes the bitter air.
The martyr, who thinks she is a female
born to the scrub board.
But then there is the casting line
with the barbed hook flashing out of the shadow.
And then there are the water walkers,
and the gauze of dragonflies.
The blind grow inconsistent.
Words like midges swarming in a cloud
move between the clotheslines
where the flycatchers twitch their tails.
They gather them with a snap
of their darling beaks.
Or, like the sperm whale's fabulous sieve of baleen,
feed on the microcosm of the world.

Living in the Past

The architect who designed the building
was avant-garde.
The American women had bobbed their hair,
Einstein had published his formulas,
the First World War had passed away.
"Let the kitchens all be here," he said in graph,
"and the stairs, one to each section."
The plantings were to be topiary.
Each five rooms had large ample windows,
baseboard hot-water heat.
An almost divine kitchen.
The fittings all Art Nouveau.
This prescient designer did not know
that by 1999 CVS would arrive
on a cement plaza outside the kitchen windows;
while skirting the plaza along Riverside Drive,
the same black metal fence enclosing
the same graveyard, the black stencil
of junipers and jackknife pines piercing
the light background of polluted air.
The new age parking lot that serves
the plaza and CVS, a vast tar-cement
square block that fills up each day
with fumes and cars. This 20s
apartment: two-story, flat-roofed,
wood, with brick facing, the units
arranged extravagantly like the letter
F in various positions. With only one side

abutting; each unit, the complete
thickness of the building.
This holdover from the rim of a naive
industrial time; a sweet moment
before the vast rush, like a total eclipse,
of the Corporate Cyclops.

Margaret Street

In September Margaret Street
waits for the comet.
No one but the earth knows that it is coming.

And the earth with its extravagant garment
like Salome's veils
gyrates in the sensual clasp.

In September the deepest basins
gush up their silt.
On Margaret Street the neighbors take out their trash.

It is Sunday. Each delayed moment
is wrested out of the seething mass.

On Mitchell Ave, where vision was still brilliant,
I suffered small indignities.
Ignorance lies always in the past.

O language that follows like the comet's tail;
the rubble of senseless longing
for what was.

Man on the Ice

Across the street, up on a roof
with a snow shovel, a man is literally
on a crevasse in the Alps. Sooner or
later he will slip, and then we
will be calling the ambulance.
How many sank in the ice floes
in those endless seasons, in the slow
going from glacier to glacier?

He is still sticking on the slope.
His aluminum ladder leaning out of reach.
As the shoveled snow sheers off,
he gets cockier; doesn't bother to grip
the clapboard, stands looking
noble, manly, useful, and ready for
a beer. This is when he starts to slip.
He has shoveled down to raw ice.
He has painted himself in, as it were.
When he slips, abruptly he sits down
to consider his options. Stay here or go
over the edge? He doesn't know it but
the same slow thought process
of some thick-skulled hairy ancestor
is slowly trickling through him
like the cold trickle of water
from a melting glacier.

March 2003

In March exact shadows on snow,
blue in the spectrum overtakes lavender;
the pillows of vapor at a slow bedroom gallop.

Up, up, the whistle pierces; the burn
of one and one, couples the rising
yearn, twin, twine, dare,
and thickening flash in shoals.

Even deep-rooted conifers,
their green wax fangs open,
hustling in the languorous swells.

What Is a Poem?

Such slight changes in air pressure,
tongue and palate,
and the differences in teeth.
Transparent words.
Why do I want to say ochre,
or what is green-yellow?
The sisters of those leaves on the ground
still lisp on the branches.
Why do I want to imitate them?

Having come this far
with a handful of alphabet,
I am forced,
with these few blocks,
to invent the universe.

Menty Ears Ago

Menty ears ago the dummer was sappy in my harms
but I was yawning and spawning and twenty.
What tears I let down in my beers of plenty.
What sleet in his goat's beard tickled my sweat.
Not a fret left its own key, every morning
when we were ferning and fronding and yorning.

My Mother's Phlox

for Ingrid

To send this to you toward the end of summer,
I was forced to rebuild my desktop.
Not in the old-fashioned way,
with saw and eye laid alongside the board
with some rue in my fingers,
that is, a slight tremble due
to anxiety and missing that former expertise;
but I wanted to create phlox.
Although, god knows, it can't be done
in three dimensions, as the earth
has so easily done it, but who can compete
with the earth? No, I wanted only the words
and they have lost themselves in the fields
or along the gravel road. It's just as well.
(*floks*) *n. pl. various plants of the genus Phlox,*
having opposite leaves and flowers,
with variously colored salverform corolla.
Over the years the phlox have spread
even into the fields beyond the barn,
into the edge of the woods, inventions
of themselves in endless designs,
now getting ragged and crepey as
the firm flesh will when it goes on too long.
But what is too long? These phlox
linger at the edges of the lawn. They exhale
their faint perfume summer after summer,
and summer after summer it was my nightlong
intoxicant. It was my potion, my ragged butterfly,

my faulty memory of my mother
who was the same age then, as I am now.
As then, I was the same age you are now,
when my mother planted these phlox in my garden.
I'm sending them to you by UPS,
wrapped in plastic in a proper box.
Take them out and stick them in water;
dig a good bed and spread the roots.
They need almost no care.
They cast their seed; they thrive on neglect.
Later they change like the faces you love,
ravaged and ravishing from year to year.

The Wailing Wall

On and off the air spits a little snow.
This changed water is so beautiful.
I think your bones are also beautiful.
Remote body, trembling with the rush
of traffic; body of altered elements.
You are my beggar's sack, the weight
of this slipping shadow, this eclipse.
You evaporate as these words evaporate.

Crows pump the air across this space;
even they are awkward in the cold.
Their grace disintegrates but not like yours.
Not yet. Another spit of snow. The lines
of chaos, fractal patterns, atmosphere.
This change of shape, this change of entity,
a strangeness like the way I miss your feet,
the way my feet loved your feet in our bed.
The way I have no bed, no resting place.

On the Dangerous Way

In the white-flocked woods, shy trash,
like trillium. Late snow speckles the raw
mud lots. Big earthmovers rest on their treads;
Archaeopteryx among guinea hens.

Slap of tires on slush and low click of termites
sucking stumps in the great cut forests;
passing methane gas.
Frost billows from a long brotherhood of trucks.

Eyes closed, the Chinese painting unrolls.
Tenuous bridge over mist to mountain;
one hairline path along the precipitous edge.
A single traveler climbs in the blowing snow.

Negative

My taste of old-fashioned wolf
in wolf's clothing,
a man like all other men
that I never knew;
if I could remember your name,
as the negative fresh from the acid
and into the fixer,
the way I remember the hard
lab table where you pushed me down
and pulled off my skirt.
Or the picnic; your basket
of thin-sliced sandwiches,
and the way you discovered
my breasts weren't nubile;
and I bicycled back
on the powdered road, unfit
to be touched by your hard,
burned hands, the bleached hairs
on your arms; your Princeton
assurance going to wrack and ruin
in the cornfields of Illinois.

On the Outer Banks

Dark over the sound,
as my love's hand,
slants the rain;
bringing to land
the grief of uprooted things;
the tremble of hung
veins, puffed black
and burst,
of long weeds
still dashed, still
upward lifted,
still downward smashed.

Pamphlet for Bullfrogs

"O solo me oh," sang a gifted bullfrog on a dark spring evening.
His bass notes trembled with heavy importunance.
Many damsel frogs were jumping after mosquitoes.
"Hmm," said one damsel to another damsel,
"let's dive down and sit on the bottom.
It's getting noisy up here."
"What these frog experts don't tell us," said one bachelor,
"is how to handle the bull. Know what I mean?
Now you take my great-grandfather,
croaked right after his nuptials."
"When I was a tad didn't have no more to worry about
than them wading herons," said another
as he leaped after the departing damsels.
"It's all froth on the beer," rumbled a puffed-out chest.
"Now all together, fellows,
let's give them a chorus they won't forget.
A one two, a one two... for he's a jolly green bellow
that nobody can but fry."

Pigs in Crisis

Poor Pitch Pig could not throw the turnip very far.
He and his sister had only one turnip between them
and someone was always taking a bite out of it.
"You did it," Poor Pitch said to Rosa. Rosa only sniffed.
Over the fence there was a beautiful field of turnips.
There was a saying in their family, "Big pig, little pig,
root hog or die." Poor Pitch Pig wondered what that meant.
He asked Rosa. Rosa looked mysterious. "Mmmmm," she said.
The farmer was far away sharpening his tools.
The farmer's daughter, who used to feed them
with baby bottles of milk when they were piglets,
often came to the pig pen to see how they were doing.
She would scratch Poor Pitch under his first chin,
saying, "Poor Pitch Pig, you are getting another chin."
Rosa never trusted the farmer's daughter.
"It's your turn to throw the turnip," she said, going to her corner.
Poor Pitch stared into the turnip field dreamily.
"If I were very small," he said, "I could slip through the wire fence.
How do I shrink myself?" Quite unexpectedly a pig fairy
gave him a kiss and Poor Pitch turned into a sow beetle.
"Rosa, Rosa," he shouted, "I'm going through the fence."
Sure enough Poor Pitch emerged in the turnip field
and turned back into himself. "Hide," cried Rosa,
"here comes the daughter." Poor Pitch wedged his way
among the leafy stalks of turnips. The wind rippled
across the field. He was gone. It was up to Rosa
to divert the farmer's daughter from her brother's plight.
Rosa went to meet the daughter, who had a nice carrot

in her hand. Rosa held up her chin bravely to be scratched.
The farmer's daughter gave her the carrot
and then she said, "Poor Piggy, you are shaking.
Do you have the ague? We must take you to the vet,"
and she got a leash and led Rosa away.
Meanwhile Poor Pitch was stuffing himself on turnip
greens. He was such a pig that he began to get sick.
The pig fairy looked at him. "You're a mess," she said.
"If I show you how to throw a turnip into right field
will you be willing to play out your role as a pig in a pen?"
Poor Pitch Pig snuffled. "Yes," he said. "I miss Rosa."
He woke up inside the pen. But Rosa was not there.
Poor Pitch Pig wept. He knew now that Rosa had never
been the one who bit the turnip ball. "I was the culprit,"
he said, and stood sadly by the trough and ate
only a little bit of the slops. Even his appetite was gone.
In a little while Rosa returned from the vet's. She was
shiny and clean and more beautiful than ever.
"My true twin sister," Poor Pitch cried squealing.
"Let me show you how to throw the turnip," he said kindly.
"By the way, where were you?" Rosa blushed.
"Went to the doctor's," she said. "I might be going to have piglets."
Poor Pitch threw the turnip thoughtfully.
"But not this year," Rosa said. "When I get bigger.
In fact," she said, "I have a date with a hog.
These few remaining months of my adolescence,"
Rosa murmured, "I will strive to be a good sister.
We will play toss the turnip, kick the turnip, roll on the turnip,

and hide the turnip as much as you like."
At that moment the farmer came to the pen.
He was carrying a very pink young pig in his arms.
"Here you go," he said, putting her in the pen.
Poor Pitch Pig blushed. It was Nelly from the next farm.
"Here," Poor Pitch said hoarsely. "Here, Nelly, eat the turnip."

Praise

Several moons ago I followed my footprints in the snow,
and it was ice and water I conversed with.
Or I said to the low moon,
ready to string up in the pale-edged sky,
"Why am I alone with you?"
And the water said,
"If the water walkers are asleep, why aren't you?"
And the dark rocks at the water's edge
tuned their frost-cracked lumps,
their blind wordless praise of dumb things.

Mindless

My mother would look in the mirror
and say, "That's not me.
I don't know that woman."
I would laugh,
with my arms around her.
I, her mindless parasite;
her wasp on the caterpillar.
In the long summer mornings
she was in the kitchen.
Slowly in my sleep,
her voice below the stairs,
singing a hymn.
And I would stir
under the light cover.
The batiste curtains at the window
lifting and sighing
in the insensible sinews of the air.

Pulsing

For the owl, meaning must coincide
with cilia in the ears,
while reality faints between its talons.
Yet for the long body stretched
on man-made fibers,
the touch-lamp is no miracle.

The threads of the sculptured carpet
or the rubbery cells of sea palm,
that sudden army rising like the drowned,
beat in rhythm to the thicker blood.

Sharing the same tendency
for flaky sweetness in the flesh,
purple shore crabs. And the couple
stirring in the bed, tending
the electric flicker in their brains,
desire only the other's tongue and sweat.

Shark

If we are born to be hungry
and we winter in the Southern
Sea, one third of our white body
filled with teeth, how can we know
what we eat is forbidden? The Gates
of Eden never closed on us. The salt
smell and the ferocious elegant tail,
not like the enamored squid, in the night
of frenzy, or the huge-brained octopus
between the narrow windings, a scroll
of rocks, intricate as illuminated pages
of the original manuscript. The holy
word of the beginning. Ah, but
so much was lost.

Spin

This slight difference in the neuron spin,
a fraction of a fraction of the whole;
that tiny tremor of the universe,
or this slight scarring of the lens in the left eye.
O trivial differences.
Sometimes you win,
sometimes you are so poor.
But what could be worse
than nothing that thinks it's something,
or the reverse?

The Driveway

Asphalt is a kind of urban lava flow
that creeps from plot to plot along a street;
affluent, weedless, slow, and cancerous;
pressure from the magma populace
for easy maintenance; neat, status-symbolic,
easy to wash with the garden hose.
And by the package, quick and simple to apply,
even with a stick. In housedresses, older women
pour it from handy bucket containers.
They get down on their knees and spread it out,
often while teenage grandsons stand by, comic
replicas of rites of passage, waiting for the tar
to set, sparring male to male. Their fathers' cars,
along the curb; trunks popped up exposing chips
and beer. These women in cotton dresses, in tennis
shoes and jersey pullovers, are too old to sweat.
They sigh when they stand up and stretch. Their flesh
is dry as the clutter of deciduous leaves in the fall
which someone will ritually hose into the gutter.

Laguna

In between rocks
purple sea urchins
stain the bottom —
lavender shingle,
strands of rose blue weeds,
a minuscule starfish,
red knobs, fringed
with underpins of blushing suckers.
Shells hang lightly moored to moss,
brown seaweed smacked down
in wet rubbery ribbons,
bloated floaters,
strands of whiskery hair,
black bristly lichen on sea-pocked rocks.
Deep-rooted supine kelp lifts up
inside the green rolling in-swell,
for a long moment appearing
like a row of dark beseeching bodies
pressed between translucent sheets of glass.
The solid green swell rolls over,
becomes bodiless in foam,
disappearing in sparks on the rocks —
spreads out to a shadow of the tide,
marking the sand in long scallops,
sliding back into itself
with a lisping whisper.

Storage

The human animal has turned a corner.
We no longer recognize one another.
I am the old species
but I must not weep. If I weep for myself
I am twice discarded.
"Don't weep," says the old brain,
"listen – I have it all on video
at half the price."

That's Not Me

I read that the left side
reveals the true self.
My true self has been
stitched to another face.
Not even my words fit.
I listen to what the
mouth is saying,
but I write in a small
notebook —
where is the body of
this person?

Every day the transit system
is a minute later.
The driver snores.
My feet move far away
in black plastic.

At night a thief enters.
Since then, the eyes in the mirror
are not mine.
Recently the nose
is unfamiliar.

Every day I am looking
for my face
among the faces that
I pass;

for my body,
a certain comfortable
size;
my voice, that even
now is not the one
that I remember.

Tell Me

"Tell me, Ruth, how is your vision?"
"Lord," I say, "know you not how it is with me?
You who are blind to the sorrows of all things temporal,
you who are not even the wind sliding under the door;
how is it that I hear this echo,
catching even in my blind eye the death throes of a distant star?"
And you say, voiceless as the forests of the mountains
of the Sahara, of the Gobi, of the Kalahari,
"Oom, ah, swept away."

The Apex

If there could be another time like that,
when all your ancestors and all of mine
conspired to bring us together. Back there
on the savanna in the days when we touched
the earth with our palms. Whose deep-set eyes
and heavy arms shoved all those others aside?

And yet, my love, you were so delicate. The flicker
of an almost infinite lightning, the infinitely small
leaping quanta, like the tracery of the universe
that was yourself, the strangeness of the animal.

The Barrier

Give back my brilliant ignorance.
Streets where I waited for you
in light waves,
in the cones of my eyes
the color of lost rooms;
those erotic odors.
Silence among the marble columns,
clash of mesh doors,
faded pretentious paper on the walls,
where we breathed in our bodies' acrid sweat
in the abyss of longing;
where we walked naked over the cheap carpets;
those casual rooms,
those pitiless hours.

The Gift from Isfahan

It is the vegetable dyes that were gathered and pounded and mixed.
It is the sheared wool carded and twisted.
It is the eyes and the fingers of children.
It is the threads tied knot by knot.
It is the daughters who carry it to the river.
It is the river that washes the skin and sweat from the patterns.
It is folded and wrapped in old cloths and sold for too little.
It is this that goes out to bless the feet of strangers.

The Jewels

Living in hell, as I do,
the devil lies in my ear.
Violent endings, devastation,
I am either the shipped-out cargo,
listing beyond the breakwater,
or the eternal widow,
standing at the window.
Always the blinding snowstorm.
At the edge of the precipice
I look into the green canopy of the valley,
then, as far as the Oort cloud
hiding its clutter of massive rocks.
How serene and deceptive the fall of tidal air —
the vast drift downward.
Body, I said,
moment by moment we wore our jewels,
we took them every day into the sunlight,
to the blind leper
on the side of the road.

The Laying Down

When the body displaces air,
even the fat content of the cells
sprays from our patterned nostrils,
as blowholes of sperm whales.
Lying down on any mattress, curved,
as space bends
the same for that occulting star,
Einstein's little proof.
Heavy the body
with embedded mineral bones
lies down on linen spread
fine as clay in gauzy layers;
as sedimentary rock,
as fossilized shale,
as shells of brachiopods.

Orbits

At the end of October, the earth tilts.
"Where are we going?" cry the tree frogs.
"Mother, the wind is blowing."
The ignorant renovator has scraped away the topsoil;
in the ruined yard, a vole has found a potato peel.
And yet, the ice crystals of October melt in the morning;
the exhausted spider eats her old web.
And who hears the faint gonging of the sun
as it shudders into the heliosphere?
Perhaps those countless baby spiders,
sucked aloft and circling the world,
like those lost Russian astronauts.

The Leaf

When I was young and oh so new,
my mother tethered me in the blue.
What was more blue than blue?
But I was green all through and through,
and what was I to do?

When I was young and oh so green,
my mother put me in a machine,
I was the living world's machine,
and I flew, and I was green all through
and through. And what was I to do?

When I had grown a single hand,
I caught the water for the land,
and drew hammers from the blue,
and I was pounded through and through,
yes, my machine created you,
and what was I to do?

When I was brittle and very old
my mother turned me into gold
and red and ochre, too.
And dropped me down with her *lu-lu-lu*;
and drained my naked veins, like you,
and I was transparent through and through,
and what was I to do?

The Old Story

Sunlight winks on enamel of dead cars.
The car dump edges a field.
At the center of this flat rush to the horizon,
one house, six bare trees, a barn, a shed.
You feel the energy of dry soil sucked into it.
An ogre lives there with his wife.
Presently they will come out to knife the earth.
A muttering robot will spread a stink of mineral powders.
A dragging rake will scrape the mortgaged furrows.
Patented cylinders will drop the beans.
The beans will grow into another world.

The Sadness of Lies

All we alienated cut-off creatures in North America
rub ourselves on patios and drink Almaden wine.
Out here in Indiana some bird of passage, green
and yellow in uptailed flight, was pecked on its small
elegant head by a meteor or an owl, and it dropped,
wings fanned out, two feet from my driveway.
Was it on its way to the Amazon or the Andes,
over the wrinkles of the bald hemisphere?
Ants have already found its warm body.
I wonder if I have Spanish blood, I say.
Perhaps I am Indian. What pterodactyl mothered
my scaled hair? I lift a wineglass to my lips.
Sister, brother, with one eye open to the filled-
up September sky, where are we going?

Progress as Reported

Developer buys scenic farm in Londonderry.
Twelve condominiums planned; hotel recreation.
Twenty acres and three barns from the turn of the century.
Some residents of the road fought the development,
including Arthur Petroley of Point Rocky Cove
who owns a second home alongside the projected condo.
Petroley says he's trying to preserve something there.
(Like a foot in both worlds. Like a vegetable giant.)
So much for labels. More info. There will be tennis courts,
putting green, golf driving range, and cross-country trails.
Not open to the public. Think of it as a privilege.
The carriage house with its elegant patterned slate roof
will be moved and used as a pool house in summer,
and used as a warming hut in winter.
Regretfully, no restaurant, due to present regulations.
But, who knows?
What use is all this scenic farmland to a land without farms?
The barns were no longer efficient.
"We are optimistic," the developer said, "that we will finalize.
As of now we are ready to bulldoze."

This Is What I Think

No longer original, or even lacquer,
still, birds and sprays of blossoms.
She sends her daughter each day
to the cabinet factory.

The daughters sit with the unassembled
design impressed in the plastic.
Always a few variations
as they dip their brushes.

The colors are all from the same pots.
The finished product is fitted together,
but in another place. The painted birds
fly, however, in the old way.

It is pleasant smiling at one another.
Like girls in school, they have secrets.
But if the fragile coating chips,
there is a quick problem in how to hide it.

When the workday is ended
they stand in line
to receive their tokens.
She waits with the others,
watching their mothers coming;

her mother and the other mothers
who are coming from assembly lines.
Perhaps she will go with her mother to the market.
The guards have checked the mothers' cards.
Her mother holds out her hand and counts the tokens.
Then, they walk carefully away together.

This Day Brings a Slight Poem

Dear April in Vermont,
are you in bud with apples
or have your cluster lilacs,
with no holds barred, tricked
the wind into long whispered
lip to lip deflowering.
Perfume of the night,
breaking erotic seals, bursting
the drops of sugar sweat
that haunts the yammering wasp,
the laden breath of every living thing,
the pheromones of yearning.

This Is How It Is

I look at the gene bank,
examples by the millions,
and they won't do.
On this planet, for me,
there was only one impetuous specimen.
How angry I become
when I walk through the corridors of my dreams.
On all the beaches of the living world,
the shadows of where you were
are washed away by the tides.
Only in my skull,
night after night,
I wrestle with your obstinate ghost.
But even that is better
than this three-dimensional life
that is so boring without you.

Tools of the Psyche

On the days when I am particularly lonely
and the man in the apartment downstairs
has finally left in his bunged-up blue Chevy,
I turn it on, after my coffee, of course,
and I say, "You're a great computer."
(It's full of my words.)
Or, on the days when my cats run up
and down the hall,
and he bangs on his wall and stomps
up and down on his floor
(he's a stickler for quiet)
I sneak in and turn it on. It's
a comfort with its luminous smile
and its chiming voice.
I admit, away from it, my eyes blur,
and I feel restless, out of sorts.
But what a leap from my old electric
typewriter, which I once adored,
and was addicted to and often paused
between words for half an hour
and filled pages with revisions,
alternatives; language that hung
in the air like sheets snapping in the wind.
But now I get on with it.
I miss those revelations, the vestry quiet
of alternatives, the questions of that body
of faith that spools into consciousness.

So what. My life is wild with slippery paper.
My printouts are filling files
and shelves, and stacked on the floor,
the cats rush into them; creational chaos.
And I'm less lonely anymore.

Trying to Write

Large as this little world,
my living room,
shuttle and loom
purrs my cat.
Blind as a bat, says my doom.

But it's blue up there,
particles of false blue.
"Swear you will always love me,"
say my eyes. "Oh yes," cries the child,
who cries in the dark.

Mark the path between the jewelweed.
If my feet stutter, and the seeds scatter,
it is memory's sarcophagus.

Visions

How many visions can I understand
and still be able to see?
asked Sandra Bachman down on the sand,
tossing a red Frisbee.
The stilts ran out with the sucking tide,
the gulls circled patiently.

Hit me, shouted the man with a beard,
as he let the Frisbee pass,
flexing and pounding his barrel chest.
She punched him hard and went dipping past.
Water combed the green eelgrass;
and I walked in the simple waves that burned,
looking for bright sea-glass.

Weathering

If your barn goes down in a high wind
and you come back in the spring
to find its planks already deep in weeds,
then the phlox come up between the timbers
and stray cats raise their endless litters
under the beams.
And bindweed moves in,
and the manic eye-surgeon over-lasers your eye,
until you are like the barn,
listing and leaning toward collapse.
The land has grown into your veins
and it pulls you under.
Some primitive thing goes with you;
moment by moment in the half-dark,
the shapes of things,
the meaningless puzzle,
fitting together like the galaxies flying apart.

What She Said

When my eyes come back,
said the blind mad woman,
I'll close them every night,
and open them every morning,
like a jewel box:
opals, moonstones.
The small flat pockets around them,
like the velvet cushions
in grandmother's cedar chest,
carefully laid away
for those exact dates
that never arrive,
but are always anticipated.

Whither Weather

Whither the weather, cry the meteorologists
as they climb the mile-high wall of heat
rising from the ocean. As moisture
is sucked up, up, the meteorologists
lean out of planes and balloons, and send
down fluttering test packages.
The great mass quivers and jellies and turns
its slate-gray eyes like a playful tiger shark.
It's not too definite today, the meteorologists say,
maybe snow, maybe rain. The convection
switches its tail. It isn't quite clear yet,
the meteorologists say; but we're excited
about this new way of forecasting weather.

What They Don't Tell Us About

This asteroid fat boy is learning disabled.
There he comes to shoot up our window,
the ionosphere. "I'm here," he shouts
to his next of kin, the hard moon.
This kid is a little punk, three miles in diameter
and solid rock. He's brushed-off
leftover pie dough. He's lonely, waiting
to kiss his trashy glitter-green mom,
who let him go in the primordial dust.
"Mom, I'm here," he flashes, faint and
out of sight. Only a quarter of a parsec
out and waiting for a jog every
million years, this passing runaway
with a slingshot. How the used old
mother's head aches from the last time;
with all those great bones left over.

The Message

How is it that I am so fond of font
and yet say nothing with it?
I ride in a carriage, water buffalo
wander outside, but all I see
is he who sits beside me.
My wit construes the carriage
drawn by hand, whose hand
I do not know and yet
we go on talking, he and I,
his face in the shadow.
Where are we going, whose
rice fields dotted with bending
women, whose terraced hills
lie like a quilt in the long draft
toward sunset, or those birds
lifting through the sky, their voices
rattling as wind rattles the dry
reeds in the marshes.
I am aware and yet I am asleep.
What he is saying is clear as type,
set by hand and bound for printing.
And yet it is upside down and backward.
I press it to my body and read it
through my skin. It is the primer
of our ancestors. It says nothing
is sacred, nothing repeats.

The Cave

My mahjong eyes weep
when the sky weeps,
when color fades,
but it is the alphabet,
neat, succulent,
fresh slants of light
on the cave walls.
O skull, your hieroglyphs
shine far down
the passage,
as if the vapors
wrapped around
this spinning rock
were sweet as
lemon peel.

About the Author

Ruth Stone was born in Virginia in 1915. Her mother read Tennyson aloud while nursing her. She began writing poetry before the age of five, and since then has published twelve volumes of poetry.

In 2002, Ruth Stone won the National Book Award and the Wallace Stevens Award from the Academy of American Poets for her book *In the Next Galaxy*. She has received many other awards and honors for her work, including the National Book Critics Circle Award, a Whiting Award, and two Guggenheim Fellowships, to name a few.

After the death of her husband in 1959, she raised their three daughters alone, while teaching at many universities.

She lives in Vermont, and her daughters live nearby.

The Chinese character for poetry is made up of two parts: "word" and "temple." It also serves as pressmark for Copper Canyon Press. Founded in 1972, Copper Canyon Press remains dedicated to publishing poetry exclusively, from Nobel laureates to new and emerging authors. The Press thrives with the generous patronage of readers, writers, booksellers, librarians, teachers, students, and funders — everyone who shares the conviction that poetry invigorates the language and sharpens our appreciation of the world.

Major funding has been provided by the following organizations:

The Allen Foundation for The Arts
Lannan Foundation
National Endowment for the Arts
Washington State Arts Commission

Lannan

NATIONAL
ENDOWMENT
FOR THE ARTS

THE ALLEN FOUNDATION *for* THE ARTS

For information and catalogs:

COPPER CANYON PRESS
Post Office Box 271
Port Townsend, Washington 98368
360/385-4925
www.coppercanyonpress.org

This book is set in Electra, created by American typographer and book designer W.A. Dwiggins in 1935. The book title is set in Arepo. Book design by Valerie Brewster, Scribe Typography. Printed on archival-quality Glatfelter Author's Text by McNaughton & Gunn, Inc.